PENGUIN BOOKS

THE PEACE OF WILD THINGS

'A farmer of sorts and an artist of sorts,' WENDELL BERRY is the author of more than fifty books of poetry, fiction and essays. He has received fellowships from the Guggenheim, Lannan and Rockefeller foundations and the National Endowment for the Arts, and also the T. S. Eliot Award, the Cleanth Brooks Medal for Lifetime Achievement and the National Humanities Medal. For more than forty years, he has lived and farmed in his native Henry Country, Kentucky, with his wife, Tanya, and their children and grandchildren.

WENDELL BERRY

The Peace of Wild Things

and other poems

PENGUIN BOOKS

PENGUIN BOOKS

UK | USA | Canada | Ireland | Australia
India | New Zealand | South Africa

Penguin Books is part of the Penguin Random House group of companies
whose addresses can be found at global.penguinrandomhouse.com.

This edition first published in
Great Britain 2018

017

Typeset in 10/13.75 pt Warnock Pro by Jouve (UK), Milton Keynes
Printed and bound in Great Britain by Clays Ltd, Elcograf S.p.A.

ISBN: 978-0-141-98712-5

www.greenpenguin.co.uk

MIX
Paper from
responsible sources
FSC® C018179
www.fsc.org

Penguin Random House is committed to a
sustainable future for our business, our readers
and our planet. This book is made from Forest
Stewardship Council® certified paper.

CONTENTS

FARMING: A HANDBOOK

THE COUNTRY OF MARRIAGE

GIVEN

SABBATH POEMS

The Broken Ground

The Apple Tree

In the essential prose
of things, the apple tree
stands up, emphatic
among the accidents
of the afternoon, solvent,
not to be denied.
The grass has been cut
down, carefully
to leave the orange
poppies still in bloom;
the tree stands up
in the odor of the grass
drying. The forked
trunk and branches are
also a kind of necessary
prose – shingled with leaves,
pigment and song
imposed on the blunt
lineaments of fact, a foliage
of small birds among them.
The tree lifts itself up
in the garden, the
clutter of its green
leaves halving the light,
stating the unalterable
congruity and form
of its casual growth;
the crimson finches appear
and disappear, singing
among the design.

An Architecture

Like a clear room, the clear stanza
of birdsong opens among the noises
of motors and breakfasts.

Among the light's beginnings,
lifting broken gray of the night's
end, the bird hastens to his song

as to a place, a room commenced
at the end of sleep. Around
him his singing is entire.

Canticle

for Robert Hazel

What death means is not this –
the spirit, triumphant in the body's fall,
praising its absence, feeding on music.
If life can't justify and explain itself,
death can't justify and explain it.
A creed and a grave never did equal the life
of anything. Yellow flowers sprout in the clefts
of ancient stones at the beginning of April.
The black clothes of the priests are turned
against the frail yellow of sunlight and petal;
they wait in their blackness to earn joy
by dying. They trust that nothing holy is free,
and so their lives are paid. Money slots
in the altar rails make a jukebox of the world,
the mind paying its gnawed coins for the safety of ignorance.

The Wild

In the empty lot – a place
not natural, but wild – among
the trash of human absence,

the slough and shamble
of the city's seasons, a few
old locusts bloom.

A few woods birds
fly and sing
in the new foliage

– warblers and tanagers, birds
wild as leaves; in a million
each one would be rare,

new to the eyes. A man
couldn't make a habit
of such color,

such flight and singing.
But they're the habit of this
wasted place. In them

the ground is wise. They are
its remembrance of what is.

The Fear of Darkness

The tall marigolds darken.
The baby cries
for better reasons than it knows.
The young wife walks
and walks among the shadows
meshed in the rooms.
And he sits in the doorway,
looking toward the woods,
long after the stars come out.
He feels the slow
sky turn toward him, and wait.
His birthright
is a third-hand Chevrolet,
bought for too much. 'I
floorboard the son of a bitch,
and let her go.'

The Plan

My old friend, the owner
of a new boat, stops by
to ask me to fish with him,

and I say I will – both of us
knowing that we may never
get around to it, it may be

years before we're both
idle again on the same day.
But we make a plan, anyhow,

in honor of friendship
and the fine spring weather
and the new boat

and our sudden thought
of the water shining
under the morning fog.

The Broken Ground

The opening out and out,
body yielding body:
the breaking
through which the new
comes, perching
above its shadow
on the piling up
darkened broken old
husks of itself:
and opening to flower
opening to fruit opening
to the sweet marrow
of the seed –
                    taken
from what was, from
what could have been.
What is left
is what is.

Openings

The Thought of Something Else

1.

A spring wind blowing
the smell of the ground
through the intersections of traffic,
the mind turns, seeks a new
nativity – another place,
simpler, less weighted
by what has already been.

Another place!
it's enough to grieve me –
that old dream of going,
of becoming a better man
just by getting up and going
to a better place.

2.

The mystery. The old
unaccountable unfolding.
The iron trees in the park
suddenly remember forests.
It becomes possible to think of going.

3.

– a place where thought
can take its shape
as quietly in the mind

as water in a pitcher,
or a man can be
safely without thought
– see the day begin
and lean back,
a simple wakefulness filling
perfectly
the spaces among the leaves.

To My Children, Fearing for Them

Terrors are to come. The earth
is poisoned with narrow lives.
I think of you. What you will

live through, or perish by, eats
at my heart. What have I done? I
need better answers than there are

to the pain of coming to see
what was done in blindness,
loving what I cannot save. Nor,

your eyes turning toward me,
can I wish your lives unmade
though the pain of them is on me.

March Snow

The morning lights
whiteness that has touched the world
perfectly as air.
In the whitened country
under the still fall of the snow
only the river, like a brown earth,
taking all falling darkly
into itself, moves.

The Finches

The ears stung with cold
sun and frost of dawn
in early April, comes

the song of winter finches,
their crimson bright, then
dark as they move into

and then against the light.
May the year warm them
soon. May they soon go

north with their singing
and the season follow.
May the bare sticks soon

live, and our minds go free
of the ground
into the shining of trees.

The Porch Over the River

In the dusk of the river, the wind
gone, the trees grow still –
the beautiful poise of lightness,
the heavy world pushing toward it.

Beyond, on the face of the water,
lies the reflection of another tree,
inverted, pulsing with the short strokes
of waves the wind has stopped driving.

In a time when men no longer
can imagine the lives of their sons
this is still the world –
the world of my time, the grind

of engines marking the country
like an audible map, the high dark
marked by the flight of men,
lights stranger than stars.

The phoebes cross and re-cross
the openings, alert
for what may still be earned
from the light. The whippoorwills

begin, and the frogs. And the dark
falls again, as it must.
The look of the world withdraws
into the vein of memory.

The mirrored tree, darkening, stirs
with the water's inward life. What has
made it so? – a quietness in it
no question can be asked in.

The Sycamore

for Henry Caudill

In the place that is my own place, whose earth
I am shaped in and must bear, there is an old tree growing,
a great sycamore that is a wondrous healer of itself.
Fences have been tied to it, nails driven into it,
hacks and whittles cut in it, the lightning has burned it.
There is no year it has flourished in
that has not harmed it. There is a hollow in it
that is its death, though its living brims whitely
at the lip of the darkness and flows outward.
Over all its scars has come the seamless white
of the bark. It bears the gnarls of its history
healed over. It has risen to a strange perfection
in the warp and bending of its long growth.
It has gathered all accidents into its purpose.
It has become the intention and radiance of its dark fate.
It is a fact, sublime, mystical and unassailable.
In all the country there is no other like it.
I recognize in it a principle, an indwelling
the same as itself, and greater, that I would be ruled by.
I see that it stands in its place, and feeds upon it,
and is fed upon, and is native, and maker.

The Dream

I dream an inescapable dream
in which I take away from the country
the bridges and roads, the fences, the strung wires,
ourselves, all we have built and dug and hollowed out,
our flocks and herds, our droves of machines.

I restore then the wide-branching trees.
I see growing over the land and shading it
the great trunks and crowns of the first forest.
I am aware of the rattling of their branches,
the lichened channels of their bark, the saps
of the ground flowing upward to their darkness.
Like the afterimage of a light that only by not
looking can be seen, I glimpse the country as it was.
All its beings belong wholly to it. They flourish
in dying as in being born. It is the life of its deaths.

I must end, always, by replacing
our beginning there, ourselves and our blades,
the flowing in of history, putting back what I took away,
trying always with the same pain of foreknowledge
to build all that we have built, but destroy nothing.

My hands weakening, I feel on all sides blindness
growing in the land on its peering bulbous stalks.
I see that my mind is not good enough.
I see that I am eager to own the earth and to own men.
I find in my mouth a bitter taste of money,
a gaping syllable I can neither swallow nor spit out.
I see all that we have ruined in order to have, all
that was owned for a lifetime to be destroyed forever.

Where are the sleeps that escape such dreams?

The Meadow

In the town's graveyard the oldest plot now frees itself
of sorrow, the myrtle of the graves grown wild. The last
who knew the faces who had these names are dead,
and now the names fade, dumb on the stones, wild
as shadows in the grass, clear to the rabbit and the wren.
Ungrieved, the town's ancestry fits the earth. They become
a meadow, their alien marble grown native as maple.

Against the War in Vietnam

Believe the automatic righteousness
of whoever holds office. Believe
the officials who see without doubt
that peace is assured by war, freedom
by oppression. The truth preserved by lying
becomes a lie. Believe or die.

In the name of ourselves we ride
at the wheels of our engines,
in the name of Plenty devouring all,
the exhaust of our progress falling
deadly on villages and fields
we do not see. We are prepared
for millions of little deaths.

Where are the quiet plenteous dwellings
we were coming to, the neighborly dwellings?
We see the American freedom defended
with lies, and the lies defended
with blood, the vision of Jefferson
served by the agony of children,
women cowering in holes.

In Memory: Stuart Egnal

A high wooded hill near Florence, an April
afternoon. Below, the valley farms
were still and small, stall and field
hushed in brightness. Around us the woods
woke with sound, and shadows lived
in the air and on the dry leaves. You
were drawing what we saw. Its forms
and lights reached slowly to your page.
We talked, and laughed at what we said.

Fine hours. The sort men dream
of having, and of having had. Today
while I slept I saw it all
again, and words for you came to me
as though we sat there talking still
in the quick of April. A wakening
strangeness – here in another valley
you never lived to come to – half
a dialogue, keeping on.

The Peace of Wild Things

When despair for the world grows in me
and I wake in the night at the least sound
in fear of what my life and my children's lives may be,
I go and lie down where the wood drake
rests in his beauty on the water, and the great heron feeds.
I come into the peace of wild things
who do not tax their lives with forethought
of grief. I come into the presence of still water.
And I feel above me the day-blind stars
waiting with their light. For a time
I rest in the grace of the world, and am free.

The Want of Peace

All goes back to the earth,
and so I do not desire
pride of excess or power,
but the contentments made
by men who have had little:
the fisherman's silence
receiving the river's grace,
the gardner's musing on rows.

I lack the peace of simple things.
I am never wholly in place.
I find no peace or grace.
We sell the world to buy fire,
our way lighted by burning men,
and that has bent my mind
and made me think of darkness
and wish for the dumb life of roots.

Do Not Be Ashamed

You will be walking some night
in the comfortable dark of your yard
and suddenly a great light will shine
round about you, and behind you
will be a wall you never saw before.
It will be clear to you suddenly
that you were about to escape,
and that you are guilty: you misread
the complex instructions, you are not
a member, you lost your card
or never had one. And you will know
that they have been there all along,
their eyes on your letters and books,
their hands in your pockets,
their ears wired to your bed.
Though you have done nothing shameful,
they will want you to be ashamed.
They will want you to kneel and weep
and say you should have been like them.
And once you say you are shamed,
reading the page they hold out to you,
then such light as you have made
in your history will leave you.
They will no longer need to pursue you.
You will pursue them, begging forgiveness.
They will not forgive you.
There is no power against them.
It is only candor that is aloof from them,
only an inward clarity, unashamed,
that they cannot reach. Be ready.
When their light has picked you out

and their questions are asked, say to them:
'I am not ashamed.' A sure horizon
will come around you. The heron will begin
his evening flight from the hilltop.

To a Siberian Woodsman

(after looking at some pictures in a magazine)

1.

You lean at ease in your warm house at night after supper,
listening to your daughter play the accordion. You smile
with the pleasure of a man confident in his hands, resting
after a day of long labor in the forest, the cry of the saw
in your head, and the vision of coming home to rest.
Your daughter's face is clear in the joy of hearing
her own music. Her fingers live on the keys
like people familiar with the land they were born in.

You sit at the dinner table late into the night with your son,
tying the bright flies that will lead you along the forest streams.
Over you, as your hands work, is the dream of the still pools.
     Over you is the dream
of your silence while the east brightens, birds waking close by
     you in the trees.

2.

I have thought of you stepping out of your doorway at dawn,
     your son in your tracks.
You go in under the overarching green branches of the forest
whose ways, strange to me, are well known to you as the sound
     of your own voice
or the silence that lies around you now that you have ceased to
     speak,
and soon the voice of the stream rises ahead of you, and you
     take the path beside it.

I have thought of the sun breaking pale through the mists over
   you
as you come to the pool where you will fish and of the mist
   drifting
over the water, and of the cast fly resting light on the face of the
   pool.

   3.

And I am here in Kentucky in the place I have made myself
in the world. I sit on my porch above the river that flows muddy
and slow along the feet of the trees. I hear the voices of the wren
and the yellow-throated warbler whose songs pass near the
   windows
and over the roof. In my house my daughter learns the womanhood
of her mother. My son is at play, pretending to be
the man he believes I am. I am the outbreathing of this ground.
My words are its words as the wren's song is its song.

   4.

Who has invented our enmity? Who had prescribed us
hatred of each other? Who has armed us against each other
with the death of the world? Who has appointed me such anger
that I should desire the burning of your house or the
   destruction of your children?
Who has appointed such anger to you? Who has set loose the
   thought
that we should oppose each other with the ruin of forests and
   rivers, and the silence of birds?

Who has said to us that the voices of my land shall be strange
to you, and the voices of your land strange to me?
Who has imagined that I would destroy myself in order to
destroy you,
or that I could improve myself by destroying you? Who has
imagined
that your death could be negligible to me now that I have seen
these pictures of your face?
Who has imagined that I would not speak familiarly with you,
or laugh with you, or visit in your house and go to work with
you in the forest?
And now one of the ideas of my place will be that you would
gladly talk and visit and work with me.

5.

I sit in the shade of the trees of the land I was born in.
As they are native I am native, and I hold to this place as
carefully as they hold to it.
I do not see the national flag flying from the staff of the
sycamore,
or any decree of the government written on the leaves of the
walnut,
nor has the elm bowed before the monuments or sworn the oath
of allegiance.
They have not declared to whom they stand in welcome.

6.

In the thought of you I imagine myself free of the weapons and
       the official hates that I have borne on my back like a
       hump,
and in the thought of myself I imagine you free of weapons and
       official hates,
so that if we should meet we would not go by each other
       looking at the ground like slaves sullen under their
       burdens,
but would stand clear in the gaze of each other.

7.

There is no government so worthy as your son who fishes with
       you in silence beside the forest pool.
There is no national glory so comely as your daughter whose
       hands have learned a music and go their own way on the
       keys.
There is no national glory so comely as my daughter who
       dances and sings and is the brightness of my house.
There is no government so worthy as my son who laughs, as he
       comes up the path from the river in the evening, for joy.

Farming: A Handbook

The Supplanting

When the road came, no longer bearing men,
but briars, honeysuckle, buckbush and wild grape,
the house fell to ruin, and only the old wife's daffodils
rose in spring among the wild vines to be domestic
and to keep the faith, and her peonies drenched the tangle
with white bloom. For a while in the years of its wilderness
a wayfaring drunk slept clinched to the floor there
in the cold nights. And then I came, and set fire
to the remnants of the house and shed, and let time
hurry in the flame. I fired it so that all
would burn, and watched the blaze settle on the waste
like a shawl. I knew those old ones departed
then, and I arrived. As the fire fed, I felt rise in me
something that would not bear my name – something that
                    bears us
through the flame, and is lightened of us, and is glad.

Sowing

In the stilled place that once was a road going down
from the town to the river, and where the lives of marriages grew
a house, cistern and barn, flowers, the tilted stone of borders,
and the deeds of their lives ran to neglect, and honeysuckle
and then the fire overgrew it all, I walk heavy
with seed, spreading on the cleared hill the beginnings
of green, clover and grass to be pasture. Between
history's death upon the place and the trees that would
                                have come
I claim, and act, and am mingled in the fate of the world.

To Know the Dark

To go in the dark with a light is to know the light.
To know the dark, go dark. Go without sight,
and find that the dark, too, blooms and sings,
and is traveled by dark feet and dark wings.

Winter Night Poem for Mary

As I started home after dark
I looked into the sky and saw the new moon,
an old man with a basket on his arm.
He walked among the cedars in the bare woods.
They stood like guardians, dark
as he passed. He might have been singing,
or he might not. He might have been sowing
the spring flowers, or he might not. But I saw him
with his basket, going along the hilltop.

Winter Nightfall

The fowls speak and sing, settling for the night.
The mare shifts in the bedding.
In her womb her foal sleeps and grows,
within and within and within. Her jaw grinds,
meditative in the fragrance of timothy.
Soon now my own rest will come.
The silent river flows on in the dusk, miles and miles.
Outside, the walls and on the roof and in the woods
the cold rain falls.

February 2, 1968

In the dark of the moon, in flying snow, in the dead of winter,
war spreading, families dying, the world in danger,
I walk the rocky hillside, sowing clover.

Enriching the Earth

To enrich the earth I have sowed clover and grass
to grow and die. I have plowed in the seeds
of winter grains and of various legumes,
their growth to be plowed in to enrich the earth.
I have stirred into the ground the offal
and the decay of the growth of past seasons
and so mended the earth and made its yield increase.
All this serves the dark. I am slowly falling
into the fund of things. And yet to serve the earth,
not knowing what I serve, gives a wideness
and a delight to the air, and my days
do not wholly pass. It is the mind's service,
for when the will fails so do the hands
and one lives at the expense of life.
After death, willing or not, the body serves,
entering the earth. And so what was heaviest
and most mute is at last raised up into song.

A Wet Time

The land is an ark, full of things waiting.
Underfoot it goes temporary and soft, tracks
filling with water as the foot is raised.
The fields, sodden, go free of plans. Hands
become obscure in their use, prehistoric.
The mind passes over changed surfaces
like a boat, drawn to the thought of roofs
and to the thought of swimming and wading birds.
Along the river croplands and gardens
are buried in the flood, airy places grown dark
and silent beneath it. Under the slender branch
holding the new nest of the hummingbird
the river flows heavy with earth, the water
turned the color of broken slopes. I stand
deep in the mud of the shore, a stake
planted to measure the rise, the water rising,
the earth falling to meet it. A great cottonwood
passes down, the leaves shivering as the roots
drag the bottom. I was not ready for this
parting, my native land putting out to sea.

On the Hill Late at Night

The ripe grassheads bend in the starlight
in the soft wind, beneath them the darkness
of the grass, fathomless, the long blades
rising out of the well of time. Cars
travel the valley roads below me, their lights
finding the dark, and racing on. Above
their roar is a silence I have suddenly heard,
and felt the country turn under the stars
toward dawn. I am wholly willing to be here
between the bright silent thousands of stars
and the life of the grass pouring out of the ground.
The hill has grown to me like a foot.
Until I lift the earth I cannot move.

A Standing Ground

Flee fro the prees, and dwelle with sothfastnesse;
Suffyce unto thy thyng, though hit be smal . . .

However just and anxious I have been,
I will stop and step back
from the crowd of those who may agree
with what I say, and be apart.
There is no earthly promise of life or peace
but where the roots branch and weave
their patient silent passages in the dark;
uprooted, I have been furious without an aim.
I am not bound for any public place,
but for ground of my own
where I have planted vines and orchard trees,
and in the heat of the day climbed up
into the healing shadow of the woods.
Better than any argument is to rise at dawn
and pick dew-wet red berries in a cup.

The Contrariness of the Mad Farmer

I am done with apologies. If contrariness is my
inheritance and destiny, so be it. If it is my mission
to go in at exits and come out at entrances, so be it.
I have planted by the stars in defiance of the experts,
and tilled somewhat by incantation and by singing,
and reaped, as I knew, by luck and Heaven's favor,
in spite of the best advice. If I have been caught
so often laughing at funerals, that was because
I knew the dead were already slipping away,
preparing a comeback, and can I help it?
And if at weddings I have gritted and gnashed
my teeth, it was because I knew where the bridegroom
had sunk his manhood, and knew it would not
be resurrected by a piece of cake. 'Dance,' they told me,
and I stood still, and while they stood
quiet in line at the gate of the Kingdom, I danced.
'Pray,' they said, and I laughed, covering myself
in the earth's brightnesses, and then stole off gray
into the midst of a revel, and prayed like an orphan.
When they said, 'I know that my Redeemer liveth,'
I told them, 'He's dead.' And when they told me,
'God is dead,' I answered, 'He goes fishing every day
in the Kentucky River. I see Him often.'
When they asked me would I like to contribute
I said no, and when they had collected
more than they needed, I gave them as much as I had.
When they asked me to join them I wouldn't,
and then went off by myself and did more
than they would have asked. 'Well, then,' they said,
'go and organize the International Brotherhood
of Contraries,' and I said, 'Did you finish killing
everybody who was against peace?' So be it.

Going against men, I have heard at times a deep harmony
thrumming in the mixture, and when they ask me what,
I say I don't know. It is not the only or the easiest
way to come to the truth. It is one way.

The Farmer and the Sea

The sea always arriving,
hissing in pebbles, is breaking
its edge where the landsman
squats on his rock. The dark
of the earth is familiar to him,
close mystery of his source
and end, always flowering
in the light and always
fading. But the dark of the sea
is perfect and strange,
the absence of any place,
immensity on the loose.
Still, he sees it is another
keeper of the land, caretaker,
shaking the earth, breaking it,
clicking the pieces, but somewhere
holding deep fields yet to rise,
shedding its richness on them
silently as snow, keeper and maker
of places wholly dark. And in him
something dark applauds.

Awake at Night

Late in the night I pay
the unrest I owe
to the life that has never lived
and cannot live now.
What the world could be
is my good dream
and my agony when, dreaming it,
I lie awake and turn
and look into the dark.
I think of a luxury
in the sturdiness and grace
of necessary things, not
in frivolity. That would heal
the earth, and heal men.
But the end, too, is part
of the pattern, the last
labor of the heart:
to learn to lie still,
one with the earth
again, and let the world go.

The Heron

While the summer's growth kept me
anxious in planted rows, I forgot the river
where it flowed, faithful to its way,
beneath the slope where my household
has taken its laborious stand.
I could not reach it even in dreams.
But one morning at the summer's end
I remember it again, as though its being
lifts into mind in undeniable flood,
and I carry my boat down through the fog,
over the rocks, and set out.
I go easy and silent, and the warblers
appear among the leaves of the willows,
their flight like gold thread
quick in the live tapestry of the leaves.
And I go on until I see, crouched
on a dead branch sticking out of the water,
a heron – so still that I believe
he is a bit of drift hung dead above the water.
And then I see the articulation of feather
and living eye, a brilliance I receive
beyond my power to make, as he
receives in his great patience
the river's providence. And then I see
that I am seen. Still as I keep,
I might be a tree for all the fear he shows.
Suddenly I know I have passed across
to a shore where I do not live.

The Country of Marriage

The Old Elm Tree by the River

Shrugging in the flight of its leaves,
it is dying. Death is slowly
standing up in its trunk and branches
like a camouflaged hunter. In the night
I am wakened by one of its branches
crashing down, heavy as a wall, and then
lie sleepless, the world changed.
That is a life I know the country by.
Mine is a life I know the country by.
Willing to live and die, we stand here,
timely and at home, neighborly as two men.
Our place is changing in us as we stand,
and we hold up the weight that will bring us down.
In us the land enacts its history.
When we stood it was beneath us, and was
the strength by which we held to it
and stood, the daylight over it
a mighty blessing we cannot bear for long.

Kentucky River Junction

to Ken Kesey & Ken Babbs

Clumsy at first, fitting together
the years we have been apart,
and the ways.

But as the night
passed and the day came, the first
fine morning of April,

it came clear:
the world that has tried us
and showed us its joy

was our bond
when we said nothing.
And we allowed it to be

with us, the green
shining.

*

Our lives, half gone,
stay full of laughter.

Free-hearted men
have the world for words.

Though we have been
apart, we have been together.

*

Trying to sleep, I cannot
take my mind away.
The bright day

shines in my head
like a coin
on the bed of a stream.

*

You left
your welcome.

Manifesto: The Mad Farmer Liberation Front

Love the quick profit, the annual raise,
vacation with pay. Want more
of everything ready-made. Be afraid
to know your neighbors and to die.
And you will have a window in your head.
Not even your future will be a mystery
any more. Your mind will be punched in a card
and shut away in a little drawer.
When they want you to buy something
they will call you. When they want you
to die for profit they will let you know.
So, friends, every day do something
that won't compute. Love the Lord.
Love the world. Work for nothing.
Take all that you have and be poor.
Love somebody who does not deserve it.
Denounce the government and embrace
the flag. Hope to live in that free
republic for which it stands.
Give your approval to all you cannot
understand. Praise ignorance, for what man
has not encountered he has not destroyed.
Ask the questions that have no answers.
Invest in the millennium. Plant sequoias.
Say that your main crop is the forest
that you did not plant,
that you will not live to harvest.
Say that the leaves are harvested
when they have rotted into the mold.
Call that profit. Prophesy such returns.
Put your faith in the two inches of humus
that will build under the trees

every thousand years.
Listen to carrion – put your ear
close, and hear the faint chattering
of the songs that are to come.
Expect the end of the world. Laugh.
Laughter is immeasurable. Be joyful
though you have considered all the facts.
So long as women do not go cheap
for power, please women more than men.
Ask yourself: Will this satisfy
a woman satisfied to bear a child?
Will this disturb the sleep
of a woman near to giving birth?
Go with your love to the fields
Lie easy in the shade. Rest your head
in her lap. Swear allegiance
to what is nighest your thoughts.
As soon as the generals and the politicos
can predict the motions of your mind,
lose it. Leave it as a sign
to mark the false trail, the way
you didn't go. Be like the fox
who makes more tracks than necessary,
some in the wrong direction.
Practice resurrection.

The Arrival

Like a tide it comes in,
wave after wave of foliage and fruit,
the nurtured and the wild,
out of the light to this shore.
In its extravagance we shape
the strenuous outline of enough.

The Wild Geese

Horseback on Sunday morning,
harvest over, we taste persimmon
and wild grape, sharp sweet
of summer's end. In time's maze
over the fall fields, we name names
that went west from here, names
that rest on graves. We open
a persimmon seed to find the tree
that stands in promise,
pale, in the seed's marrow.
Geese appear high over us,
pass, and the sky closes. Abandon,
as in love or sleep, holds
them to their way, clear,
in the ancient faith: what we need
is here. And we pray, not
for new earth or heaven, but to be
quiet in heart, and in eye
clear. What we need is here.

Anger Against Beasts

The hook of adrenaline shoves
into the blood. Man's will,
long schooled to kill or have
its way, would drive the beast
against nature, transcend
the impossible in simple fury.
The blow falls like a dead seed.
It is defeat, for beasts
do not pardon, but heal or die
in the absence of the past.
The blow survives in the man.
His triumph is a wound. Spent,
he must wait the slow
unalterable forgiveness of time.

Planting Crocuses

1.

I made an opening
to reach through blind
into time, through
sleep and silence, to new
heat, a new rising,
a yellow flower opening
in the sound of bees.

2.

Deathly was the giving
of that possibility
to a motion of the world
that would bring it
out, bright, in time.

3.

My mind pressing in
through the earth's
dark motion toward
bloom, I thought of you,
glad there is no escape.
It is this we will be
turning and re-
turning to.

Poem for J.

What she has made in her body is broken.
Now she has begun to bear it again.
In the house of her son's death
his life is shining in the windows,
for she has elected to bear him again.
She did not bear him for death,
and she does not. She has taken back
into her body the seed, bitter
and joyous, of the life of a man.

In the house of the dead the windows shine
with life. She mourns, for his life was good.
She is not afraid. She is like a field
where the corn is planted, and like the rain
that waters the field, and like the young corn.
In her sorrow she renews life, in her grief
she prepares the return of joy.

She did not bear him for death, and she does not.
There was a life that went out of her to live
on its own, divided, and now she has taken it back.
She is alight with the sudden new life of death.
Perhaps it is the brightness of the dead one
being born again. Perhaps she is planting him,
like corn, in the living and in the earth.
She has taken back into her flesh,
and made light, the dark seed of her pain.

Clearing

History

For Wallace Stegner

1.

The crops were made, the leaves
were down, three frosts had lain
upon the broad stone
step beneath the door;
as I walked away
the houses were shut, quiet
under their drifting smokes,
the women stooped at the hearths.
Beyond the farthest tracks
of any domestic beast
my way led me, into
a place for which I knew
no names. I went by paths
that bespoke intelligence
and memory I did not know.
Noonday held sounds of moving
water, moving air, enormous
stillness of old trees.
Though I was weary and alone,
song was near me then,
wordless and gay as a deer
lightly stepping. Learning
the landmarks and the ways
of that land, so I might
go back, if I wanted to,
my mind grew new, and lost
the backward way. I stood
at last, long hunter and child,

where this valley opened,
a word I seemed to know
though I had not heard it.
Behind me, along the crooks
and slants of my approach,
a low song sang itself,
as patient as the light.
On the valley floor the woods
grew rich: great poplars,
beeches, sycamores,
walnuts, sweet gums, lindens,
oaks. They stood apart
and open, the winter light
at rest among them. Yes,
and as I came down
I heard a little stream
pouring into the river.

2.

Since then I have arrived here
many times. I have come
on foot, on horseback, by boat,
and by machine — by earth,
water, air and fire.
I came with axe and rifle.
I came with a sharp eye
and the price of land. I came
in bondage, and I came
in freedom not worth the name.
From the high outlook

of that first day I have come
down two hundred years
across the worked and wasted
slopes, by eroding tracks
of the joyless horsepower of greed.
Through my history's despite
and ruin, I have come
to its remainder, and here
have made the beginning
of a farm intended to become
my art of being here.
By it I would instruct
my wants: they should belong
to each other and to this place.
Until my song comes here
to learn its words, my art
is but the hope of song.

3.

All the lives this place
has had, I have. I eat
my history day by day.
Bird, butterfly, and flower
pass through the seasons of
my flesh. I dine and thrive
on offal and old stone,
and am combined within
the story of the ground.
By this earth's life, I have
its greed and innocence,

its violence, its peace.
Now let me feed my song
upon the life that is here
that is the life that is gone.
This blood has turned to dust
and liquefied again in stem
and vein ten thousand times.
Let what is in the flesh,
O Muse, be brought to mind

A Part

To my mother, who gave me books

Stay Home

I will wait here in the fields
to see how well the rain
brings on the grass.
In the labor of the fields
longer than a man's life
I am home. Don't come with me.
You stay home too.

I will be standing in the woods
where the old trees
move only with the wind
and then with gravity.
In the stillness of the trees
I am at home. Don't come with me.
You stay home too.

The Cold Pane

Between the living world
and the world of death
is a clear, cold pane;
a man who looks too close
must fog it with his breath,
or hold his breath too long.

A Meeting

In a dream I meet
my dead friend. He has,
I know, gone long and far,
and yet he is the same
for the dead are changeless.
They grow no older.
It is I who have changed,
grown strange to what I was.
Yet I, the changed one,
ask: 'How you been?'
He grins and looks at me.
'I been eating peaches
off some mighty fine trees.'

Another Descent

Through the weeks of deep snow
we walked above the ground
on fallen sky, as though we did
not come of root and leaf, as though
we had only air and weather
for our difficult home.
                              But now
as March warms, and the rivulets
run like birdsong on the slopes,
and the branches of light sing in the hills,
slowly we return to earth.

Below

Above trees and rooftops
is the range of symbols:
banner, cross, and star;
air war, the mode of those
who live by symbols; the pure
abstraction of travel by air.
Here a spire holds up
an angel with trump and wings;
he's in *his* element.
Another lifts a hand
with forefinger pointing up
to admonish that all's not here.
All's not. But I aspire
downward. Flyers embrace
the air, and I'm a man
who needs something to hug.
All my dawns cross the horizon
and rise, from underfoot.
What I stand for
is what I stand on.

Ripening

The longer we are together
the larger death grows around us.
How many we know by now
who are dead! We, who were young,
now count the cost of having been.
And yet as we know the dead
we grow familiar with the world.
We, who were young and loved each other
ignorantly, now come to know
each other in love, married
by what we have done, as much
as by what we intend. Our hair
turns white with our ripening
as though to fly away in some
coming wind, bearing the seed
of what we know. It was bitter to learn
that we come to death as we come
to love, bitter to face
the just and solving welcome
that death prepares. But that is bitter
only to the ignorant, who pray
it will not happen. Having come
the bitter way to better prayer, we have
the sweetness of ripening. How sweet
to know you by the signs of this world!

Fall

for Wallace Fowlie

The wild cherries ripen, black and fat,
Paradisal fruits that taste of no man's sweat.

Reach up, pull down the laden branch, and eat;
When you have learned their bitterness, they taste sweet.

Throwing Away the Mail

Nothing is simple,
not even simplification.
Thus, throwing away
the mail, I exchange
the complexity of duty
for the simplicity of guilt.

For the Future

Planting trees early in spring,
we make a place for birds to sing
in time to come. How do we know?
They are singing here now.
There is no other guarantee
that singing will ever be.

Traveling at Home

Even in a country you know by heart
it's hard to go the same way twice.
The life of the going changes.
The chances change and make a new way.
Any tree or stone or bird
can be the bud of a new direction. The
natural correction is to make intent
of accident. To get back before dark
is the art of going.

The Slip

for Donald Davie

The river takes the land, and leaves nothing.
Where the great slip gave way in the bank
and an acre disappeared, all human plans
dissolve. An aweful clarification occurs
where a place was. Its memory breaks
from what is known now, begins to drift.
Where cattle grazed and trees stood, emptiness
widens the air for birdflight, wind, and rain.
As before the beginning, nothing is there.
Human wrong is in the cause, human
ruin in the effect – but no matter;
all will be lost, no matter the reason.
Nothing, having arrived, will stay.
The earth, even, is like a flower, so soon
passeth it away. And yet this nothing
is the seed of all – the clear eye
of Heaven, where all the worlds appear.
Where the imperfect has departed, the perfect
begins its struggle to return. The good gift
begins again its descent. The maker moves
in the unmade, stirring the water until
it clouds, dark beneath the surface,
stirring and darkening the soul until pain
perceives new possibility. There is nothing
to do but learn and wait, return to work
on what remains. Seed will sprout in the scar.
Though death is in the healing, it will heal.

The Wheel

Rising

for Kevin Flood

1.

Having danced until nearly
time to get up, I went on
in the harvest, half lame
with weariness. And he
took no notice, and made
no mention of my distress.
He went ahead, assuming
that I would follow. I followed,
dizzy, half blind, bitter
with sweat in the hot light.
He never turned his head,
a man well known by his back
in those fields in those days.
He led me through long rows
of misery, moving like a dancer
ahead of me, so elated
he was, and able, filled
with desire for the ground's growth.
We came finally to the high
still heat of four o'clock,
a long time before sleep.
And then he stood by me
and looked at me as I worked,
just looked, so that my own head
uttered his judgment, even
his laughter. He only said:
'That social life doesn't get
down the row, does it, boy?'

2.

I worked by will then, he
by desire. What was ordeal
for me, for him was order
and grace, ideal and real.

That was my awkward boyhood,
the time of his mastery.
He troubled me to become
what I had not thought to be.

3.

The boy must learn the man
whose life does not travel
along any road, toward
any other place,
but is a journey back and forth
in rows, and in the rounds
of years. His journey's end
is no place of ease, but the farm
itself, the place day labor
starts from, journeys in,
returns to: the fields
whose past and potency are one.

4.

And that is our story,
not of time, but the forever

returning events of light,
ancient knowledge seeking
new minds. The man at dawn
in spring of the year,
going to the fields,
visionary of seed and desire,
is timeless as a star.

5.

Any man's death could end the story:
his mourners, having accompanied him
to the grave through all he knew,
turn back, leaving him complete.

But this is not the story of a life.
It is the story of lives, knit together,
overlapping in succession, rising
again from grave after grave.

For those who depart from it, bearing it
in their minds, the grave is a beginning.
It has weighted the earth with sudden
new gravity, the enrichment of pain.

There is a grave, too, in each
survivor. By it, the dead one lives.
He enters us, a broken blade,
sharp, clear as a lens or a mirror.

And he comes into us helpless, tender
as the newborn enter the world. Great
is the burden of our care. We must be true
to ourselves. How else will he know us?

Like a wound, grief receives him.
Like graves, we heal over, and yet keep
as part of ourselves the severe gift.
By grief, more inward than darkness,

the dead become the intelligence of life.
Where the tree falls the forest rises.
There is nowhere to stand but in absence,
no life but in the fateful light.

6.

Ended, a story is history;
it is in time, with time
lost. But if a man's life
continues in another man,
then the flesh will rhyme
its part in immortal song.
By absence, he comes again.

There is a kinship of the fields
that gives to the living the breath
of the dead. The earth
opened in the spring, opens
in all springs. Nameless,
ancient, many-lived, we reach
through ages with the seed.

Song

I stood and heard the steps of the city
and dreamed a lighter stepping than I heard,
the tread of my people dancing in a ring.
I knew that circle broken, the steps awry,
stone and iron humming in the air.

But I thought even there, among the straying
steps, of the dance that circles life around,
its shadows moving on the ground, in rhyme
of flesh with flesh, time with time, our bliss,
the earthly song that heavenly is.

Our Children, Coming of Age

In the great circle, dancing in
and out of time, you move now
toward your partners, answering
the music suddenly audible to you
that only carried you before
and will carry you again.
When you meet the destined ones
now dancing toward you,
we will be in line behind you,
out of your awareness for the time,
we whom you know, others we remember
whom you do not remember, others
forgotten by us all.
When you meet, and hold love
in your arms, regardless of all,
the unknown will dance away from you
toward the horizon of light.
Our names will flutter
on these hills like little fires.

Entries

The Record

My old friend tells us how the country changed:
where the grist mill was on Cane Run,
now gone; where the peach orchard was,
gone too; where the Springport Road was, gone
beneath returning trees; how the creek ran three weeks
after a good rain, long ago, no more;
how when these hillsides first were plowed, the soil
was black and deep, no stones, and that was long ago;
where the wild turkeys roosted in the old days;
'You'd have to know this country mighty well
before I could tell you where.'

And my young friend says: 'Have him speak this
into a recorder. It is precious. It should be saved.'
I know the panic of that wish to save
the vital knowledge of the old times, handed down,
for it is rising off the earth, fraying away
in the wind and the coming day.
As the machines come and the people go
the old names rise, chattering, and depart.

But knowledge of my own going into old time
tells me no. Because it must be saved,
do not tell it to a machine to save it.
That old man speaking you have heard
since your boyhood, since his prime, his voice
speaking out of lives long dead, their minds
speaking in his own, by winter fires, in fields and woods,
in barns while rain beat on the roofs
and wind shook the girders. Stay and listen
until he dies or you die, for death
is in this, and grief is in it. Live here

as one who knows those things. Stay, if you live;
listen and answer. Listen to the next one
like him, if there is to be one. Be
the next one like him, if you must;
say and wait. Tell your children. Tell them
to tell their children. As you depart
toward the coming light, turn back
and speak, as the creek steps downward
over the rocks, saying the same changing thing
in the same place as it goes.

When the record is made, the unchanging
word carried to a safe place
in a time not here, the assemblage
of minds dead and living, the loved lineage
dispersed, silent, turned away, the dead
dead at last, it will be too late.

A Parting

From many hard workdays in the fields,
many passages through the woods,
many mornings on the river, lifting
hooked lines out of the dark,
from many nightfalls, many dawns,
on the ridgetops and the creek road,
as upright as a tree, as freely standing,
Arthur Rowanberry comes in his old age
into the care of doctors, into the prison
of technical mercy, disease
and hectic skill making their way
into his body, hungry invaders fighting
for claims in that dark homeland,
strangers touching him, calling his name,
and so he lies down at last
in a bare room far from home.
And we who know him come
from the places he knew us in, and stand
by his bed, and speak. He smiles
and greets us from another time.
We stand around him like a grove,
a moment's shelter, old neighborhood
remade in that alien place. But the time
we stand in is not his time.
He is off in the places of his life,
now only places in his mind,
doing what he did in them when they were
the world's places, and he the world's man:
cutting the winter wood, piling the brush,
fixing the fences, mending the roofs,
caring for the crops under the long sun,
loading up the wagon, heading home.

The Wild Rose

Sometimes hidden from me
in daily custom and in trust,
so that I live by you unaware
as by the beating of my heart,

suddenly you flare in my sight,
a wild rose blooming at the edge
of thicket, grace and light
where yesterday was only shade

and once more I am blessed, choosing
again what I chose before.

The Blue Robe

How joyful to be together, alone
as when we first were joined
in our little house by the river
long ago, except that now we know

each other, as we did not then;
and now instead of two stories fumbling
to meet, we belong to one story
that the two, joining, made. And now

we touch each other with the tenderness
of mortals, who know themselves:
how joyful to feel the heart quake

at the sight of a grandmother,
old friend in the morning light,
beautiful in her blue robe!

Let Us Pledge

Let us pledge allegiance to the flag
and to the national sacrifice areas
for which it stands, garbage dumps
and empty holes, sold out for a higher
spire on the rich church, the safety
of voyagers in golf carts, the better mood
of the stock market. Let us feast
today, though tomorrow we starve. Let us
gorge upon the body of the Lord, consuming
the earth for our greater joy in Heaven,
that fair Vacationland. Let us wander forever
in the labyrinths of our self-esteem.
Let us evolve forever toward the higher
consciousness of the machine.
The spool of our engine-driven fate
unwinds, our history now outspeeding
thought, and the heart is a beatable tool.

Come Forth

I dreamed of my father when he was old.
We went to see some horses in a field;
they were sorrels, as red almost as blood
the light gold on their shoulders and haunches.
Though they came to us, all a-tremble
with curiosity and snorty with caution,
they had never known bridle or harness.
My father walked among them, admiring,
for he was a knower of horses, and these were fine.

He leaned on a cane and dragged his feet
along the ground in hurried little steps
so that I called to him to take care, take care,
as the horses stamped and frolicked around him.
But while I warned, he seized the mane
of the nearest one. 'It'll be all right,'
he said, and then from his broken stance
he leapt astride, and sat lithe and straight
and strong in the sun's unshadowed excellence.

Given

In Memory: Ross Field

In a Country Once Forested

The young woodland remembers
the old, a dreamer dreaming

of an old holy book,
an old set of instructions,

and the soil under the grass
is dreaming of a young forest,

and under the pavement the soil
is dreaming of grass.

They

I see you down there, white-haired
among the green leaves,
picking the ripe raspberries,
and I think, 'Forty-two years!'
We are the you and I who were
they whom we remember.

Why

Why all the embarrassment
about being happy?
Sometimes I'm as happy
as a sleeping dog,
and for the same reasons,
and for others.

Listen!

How fine to have a radio
and beautiful music playing
while I sit at rest in the evening.
How fine to hear through the music
the cries of wild geese on the river.

How to be a Poet

(to remind myself)

Make a place to sit down.
Sit down. Be quiet.
You must depend upon
affection, reading, knowledge,
skill – more of each
than you have – inspiration,
work, growing older, patience,
for patience joins time
to eternity. Any readers
who like your work,
doubt their judgment.

Breathe with unconditional breath
the unconditioned air.
Shun electric wire.
Communicate slowly. Live
a three-dimensioned life;
stay away from screens.
Stay away from anything
that obscures the place it is in.
There are no unsacred places;
there are only sacred places
and desecrated places.

Accept what comes from silence.
Make the best you can of it.
Of the little words that come
out of the silence, like prayers
prayed back to the one who prays,
make a poem that does not disturb
the silence from which it came.

Sabbath Poems

I.

I go among trees and sit still.
All my stirring becomes quiet
around me like circles on water.
My tasks lie in their places
where I left them, asleep like cattle.

Then what is afraid of me comes
and lives a while in my sight.
What it fears in me leaves me,
and the fear of me leaves it.
It sings, and I hear its song.

Then what I am afraid of comes.
I live for a while in its sight.
What I fear in it leaves it,
and the fear of it leaves me.
It sings, and I hear its song.

After days of labor,
mute in my consternations,
I hear my song at last,
and I sing it. As we sing,
the day turns, the trees move.

II.

I go from the woods into the cleared field:
A place no human made, a place unmade
By human greed, and to be made again.
Where centuries of leaves once built by dying
A deathless potency of light and stone
And mold of all that grew and fell, the timeless
Fell into time. The earth fled with the rain,
The growth of fifty thousand years undone
In a few careless seasons, stripped to rock
And clay – a 'new land', truly, that no race
Was ever native to, but hungry mice
And sparrows and the circling hawks, dry thorns
And thistles sent by generosity
Of new beginning. No Eden, this was
A garden once, a good and perfect gift;
Its possible abundance stood in it
As it then stood. But now what it might be
Must be foreseen, darkly, through many lives –
Thousands of years to make it what it was,
Beginning now, in our few troubled days.

III.

In a crease of the hill
under the light,
out of the wind,
as warmth, bloom and song
return, lady, I think of you,
and of myself with you.
What are we but forms
of the self-acknowledging
light that brings us
warmth and song from time
to time? Lip and flower,
hand and leaf, tongue
and song, what are we but welcomers
of that ancient joy, always
coming, always passing?
Mayapples rising
out of old time, leaves
folded down around
the stems, as if for flight,
flower bud folded in
unfolding leaves, what
are we but hosts
of times, of all
the Sabbath morning shows,
the light that finds it good.

IV.

The year relents, and free
Of work, I climb again
To where the old trees wait,
Time out of mind. I hear
Traffic down on the road,
Engines high overhead.
And then a quiet comes,
A cleft in time, silence
Of metal moved by fire;
The air holds little voices
Titmice and chickadees,
Feeding through the treetops
Among the new small leaves,
Calling again to mind
The grace of circumstance,
Sabbath economy
In which all thought is song,
All labor is a dance.
The world is made at rest,
In ease of gravity.
I hear the ancient theme
In low world-shaping song
Sung by the falling stream.
Here where a rotting log
Has slowed the flow: a shelf
Of dark soil, level laid
Above the tumbled stone.
Roots fasten it in place.
It will be here a while;
What holds it here decays.
A richness from above,
Brought down, is held, and holds

A little while in flow.
Stem and leaf grow from it.
At cost of death, it has
A life. Thus falling founds,
Unmaking makes the world.

V.

Over the river in loud flood
in the wind deep and broad
under the unending sky, pair
by pair, the swallows again,
with tender exactitude,
play out their line
in arcs laid on the air,
as soon as made, not there.

VI.

The summer ends, and it is time
To face another way. Our theme
Reversed, we harvest the last row
To store against the cold, undo
The garden that will be undone.
We grieve under the weakened sun
To see all earth's green fountains dried,
And fallen all the works of light.
You do not speak, and I regret
This downfall of the good we sought
As though the fault were mine. I bring
The plow to turn the shattering
Leaves and bent stems into the dark,
From which they may return. At work,
I see you leaving our bright land,
The last cut flowers in your hand.

VII.

Coming to the woods' edge
on my Sunday morning walk,
I stand resting a moment beside
a ragged half-dead wild plum
in bloom, its perfume
a moment enclosing me,
and standing side by side
with the old broken blooming tree,
I almost understand,
I almost recognize as a friend
the great impertinence of beauty
that comes even to the dying,
even to the falling, without reason
sweetening the air.

                I walk on,
Distracted by a letter accusing me
of distraction, which distracts me
only from the hundred things
that would otherwise distract me
from this whiteness, lightness,
sweetness in the air. The mind
is broken by the thousand
calling voices it is always too late
to answer, and that is why it yearns
for some hard task, lifelong, longer
than life, to concentrate it
and make it whole.

But where is the all-welcoming,
all-consecrating Sabbath
that would do the same? Where

the quietness of the heart
and the eye's clarity
that would be a friend's reply
to the white-blossoming plum tree?

VIII.

Always in the distance
the sound of cars is passing
on the road, that simplest form
going only two ways,
both ways away. And I
have been there in that going.

But now I rest and am
apart, a part of the form
of the woods always arriving
from all directions home,
this cell of wild sound,
the hush of the trees, singers
hidden among the leaves –

a form whose history is old,
needful, unknown, and bright
as the history of the stars
that tremble in the sky at night
like leaves of a great tree.

IX.

In the early morning we awaken from
The sound of engines running in the night,
And then we start the engines of the day.
We speed away into the fading light.

Nowhere is any sound but of our going
On roads strung everywhere with humming wire.
Nowhere is there an end except in smoke.
This is the world that we have set on fire.

This is the promised burning, darkening
Our light of hope and putting out the sun,
Blighting the leaf, the stream – and blessed area
The dead who died before this time began.

Blessed the dead who have escaped in time
The twisted metal and the fractured stone,
The technobodies of the hopeless cure.
Now, to the living, only grief has shown

The little yellow of the violet
Risen again out of the dead year's leaves,
And grief alone is the measure of the love
That only lives by rising out of graves.

X.

The sky bright after summer-ending rain
I sat against an oak half up the climb.
The sun was low; the woods was hushed in shadow;
Now the long shimmer of the crickets' song
Had stopped. I looked up to the westward ridge
And saw the ripe October light again,
Shining through leaves still green yet turning gold.
Those glowing leaves made of the light a place
That time and leaf would leave. The wind came cool,
And then I knew that I was present in
The long age of the passing world, in which
I once was not, now am, and will not be,
And in that time, beneath the changing tree,
I rested in a keeping not my own.

XI.

To give mind to machines, they are calling it
out of the world, out of the neighborhood, out of the body.
They have bound it in the brain, in the hard shell
of the skull, in order to bind it in a machine.
From the heron flying home at dusk,
from the misty hollows at sunrise,
from the stories told at the row's end,
they are calling the mind into exile
in the dry circuits of machines.

XII.

I walk in openings
That when I'm dead will close.
Where the field sparrow sings
Will come the sweet wild rose.

The yellowthroat will claim
The tangle with his song,
The redbud and wild plum
Light up the hill in spring

Where in the morning shade
My team of horses drew
The chattering iron blade,
Their fetlocks wet with dew

Briar, bittersweet, and fern,
Box elder, locust, elm,
Cedar, wild grape, and thorn
Will reinstate the time

Of deep root and wide shadow,
Of bright, hot August calm
On the small, tree-ringed meadow
Of goldenrod and bee balm.

Thicket will grow up through
The thatches of the grass,
An old way turning new
As lives and wishes pass.

And as the thicket dies
The hickory ash, and oak

Of the true woods will rise
Across a long time, like

Will speak to like, the breeze
Resume old music in
The branch-ends of the trees,
The long age come again.

The hard field will find ease
In being thus released:
Let it grow wild in peace,
My workplace come to rest.

To speed this change of goods
I spare the seedling trees,
And thus invoke the woods,
The genius of this place;

I stop the mower blade,
And so conspire with time
In the return of shade,
Completion of this rhyme.

XIII.

The body in the invisible
Familiar room accepts the gift
Of sleep, and for a while is still;
Instead of will, it lives by drift

In the great night that gathers up
The earth and sky. Slackened, unbent,
Unwanting, without fear or hope,
The body rests beyond intent.

Sleep is the prayer the body prays,
Breathing in unthought faith the Breath
That through our worry-wearied days
Preserves our rest, and is our truth.

XIV.

The team rests in shade at the edge
of the half-harrowed field, the first
warm morning of May. Wind breathes
over the worked ground, through maples
by the creek, moving every new leaf.
The stream sings quietly in passing.
Too late for frost, too early for flies,
the air carries only birdsong, the long
draft of wind through leaves. In this time
I could stay forever. In my wish
to stay forever, it stays forever,
But I must go. Mortal and obliged,
I shake off stillness, stand and go back
to the waiting field, unending rounds.

XV.

Loving you has taught me the infinite
longing of the self to be given away
and the great difficulty of that entire
giving, for in love to give is to receive
and then there is yet more to give;
and others have been born of our giving
to whom the self, greatened by gifts,
must be given, and by that giving
be increased, until, self-burdened,
the self, staggering upward in years,
in fear, hope, love, and sorrow,
imagines, rising like a moon,
a pale moon risen in daylight
over the dark woods, the Self
whose gift we and all others are,
the self that is by definition given.

XVI.

Lift up the dead leaves
and see, waiting
in the dark, in cold March,

the purplish stems, leaves,
and buds of twinleaf,
infinitely tender, infinitely

expectant. They straighten
slowly into the light after
the nights of frost. At last

the venture is made: the brief
blossoms open, the petals fall,
the hinged capsules of seed

grow big. The possibility
of this return returns
again to the seed, the dark,

the long wait, and the light again.

XVII.

Remembering Evia
for Liadain, Denise, and Philip

We went in darkness where
We did not know or why
Or how we'd come so far
Past sight or memory.

We climbed a narrow path
Up a moon-shadowed slope.
The guide we journeyed with
Held a small light. And step

By step our shadows rose
With us, and then fell back
Before the shine of windows
That opened in the black

Hillside, or so it seemed.
We reached a windy porch
As if both seen and dreamed
On its dark, lofty perch

Between the sky and sea.
A lamplit table spread
Old hospitality
Of cheese and wine and bread.

Darker than wine, the waves
Muttered upon the stones,
Asking whose time it was,
Our time or Agamemnon's.

The sea's undying sound
Demarked a land unknown
To us, who therein found
Welcome, our travel done.

XVIII.

They sit together on the porch, the dark
Almost fallen, the house behind them dark.
Their supper done with, they have washed and dried
The dishes – only two plates now, two glasses,
Two knives, two forks, two spoons – small work for two.
She sits with her hands folded in her lap,
At rest. He smokes his pipe. They do not speak.
And when they speak at last it is to say
What each one knows the other knows. They have
One mind between them, now that finally,
For all its knowing will not exactly know
Which one goes first through the dark doorway, bidding
Goodnight, and which sits on a while alone.

XIX.

Some Sunday afternoon, it may be,
you are sitting under your porch roof,
looking down through the trees
to the river, watching the rain. The circles
made by the raindrops' striking
expand, intersect, dissolve,

and suddenly (for you are getting on
now, and much of your life is memory)
the hands of the dead, who have been here
with you, rest upon you tenderly
as the rain rests shining
upon the leaves. And you think then

(for thought will come) of the strangeness
of the thought of Heaven, for now
you have imagined yourself there,
remembering with longing this
happiness, this rain. Sometimes here
we are there, and there is no death.

XX.

Even while I dreamed I prayed that what I saw was only fear
        and no foretelling,
for I saw the last known landscape destroyed for the sake
of the objective, the soil bulldozed, the rock blasted.
Those who had wanted to go home would never get there
        now.

I visited the offices where for the sake of the objective the
        planners planned
at blank desks set in rows. I visited the loud factories
where the machines were made that would drive ever
        forward
toward the objective. I saw the forest reduced to stumps and
        gullies; I saw
the poisoned river, the mountain cast into the valley;
I came to the city that nobody recognized because it looked
        like every other city.
I saw the passages worn by the unnumbered
footfalls of those whose eyes were fixed upon the objective.

Their passing had obliterated the graves and the
        monuments
of those who had died in pursuit of the objective
and who had long ago forever been forgotten, according
to the inevitable rule that those who have forgotten forget
that they have forgotten. Men, women, and children now
        pursued the objective
as if nobody ever had pursued it before.
The races and the sexes now intermingled perfectly in
        pursuit of the objective.

The once-enslaved, the once-oppressed were now free
to sell themselves to the highest bidder
and to enter the best-paying prisons
in pursuit of the objective, which was the destruction of all
       enemies,
which was the destruction of all obstacles, which was the
       destruction of all objects,
which was to clear the way to victory which was to clear the
       way to promotion, to salvation, to progress,
to the completed sale, to the signature
on the contract, which was to clear the way
to self-realization, to self-creation, from which nobody who
       ever wanted to go home
would ever get there now, for every remembered place
had been displaced; the signposts had been bent to the
       ground and covered over.
Every place had been displaced, every love
unloved, every vow unsworn, every word unmeant
to make way for the passage of the crowd
of the individuated, the autonomous, the self-actuated,
       the homeless
with their many eyes opened only toward the objective
which they did not yet perceive in the far distance,
having never known where they were going,
having never known where they came from.

XXI.

I was wakened from my dream of the ruined world by the
        sound
of rain falling slowly onto the dry earth of my place in time.
On the parched garden, the cracked-open pastures,
the dusty grape leaves, the brittled grass, the drooping
        foliage of the woods,
fell still the quiet rain.

XXII.

There is a day
when the road neither
comes nor goes, and the way
is not a way but a place.

XXIII.

The watcher comes, knowing the small
knowledge of his life in this body
in this place in this world. He comes
to a place of rest where he cannot
mistake himself as larger than he is,
the place of the gray flycatcher,
the yellow butterfly, the green dragonfly,
the white violet, the columbine,
where he cannot mistake himself
as more graced or graceful than he is.

At the woods' edge, the wild rose
is in bloom, beauty and consolation
always in excess of thought.

XXIV.

The year falls also from
the human-borne plagues
that kill the trees, foul
the air, the water, and the earth,
bringing to the world the curse
of frivolous death, the tiresome
novelty of wastefulness,
the ugly forethoughtfulness of fear.

What repair, what
return, will undo the consuming
self-belittlement that inherits,
disvalues, neglects and ruins
the decent small farm –
the earned, kept, and cherished
good of a lifetime's work
gone – to break the heart?

And yet the light comes.
And yet the light is here.
Over the long shadows
the late light moves
in beauty through the living woods.

ACKNOWLEDGEMENTS

The poems in this collection were originally published in the following:

    The Broken Ground (New York: Harcourt, Brace & World, 1964)
    Openings (New York: Harcourt, Brace & World, 1968)
    Farming: A Handbook (New York: Harcourt,
        Brace & World, 1970)
    The Country of Marriage (New York: Harcourt,
        Brace & World, 1973)
    Clearing (New York: Harcourt, Brace & World, 1977)
    A Part (San Francisco: North Point Press, 1980)
    The Wheel (San Francisco: North Point Press, 1982)
    Entries (Washington, D.C.: Counterpoint, 1994)
    A Timbered Choir: The Sabbath Poems, 1979–1997
        (New York: Counterpoint, 1999)
    Given (Berkeley: Counterpoint, 2005)
    A Small Porch: Sabbath Poems 2014
        (Berkeley: Counterpoint, 2016)

The poems in this collection are also available in the following Counterpoint Press US editions:

    A Timbered Choir: The Sabbath Poems, 1979–1997
        (New York: Counterpoint, 1999)
    New Collected Poems (Berkeley: Counterpoint, 2012)
    A Small Porch: Sabbath Poems 2014 (Berkeley: Counterpoint, 2016)